LOST STAR

The Story of Amelia Earhart

LOST STAR

The Story of Amelia Earhart

by Patricia Lauber

SCHOLASTIC INC.
New York Toronto London Auckland Sydney

Book and cover design by Georgia Morrissey.

ISBN 0-590-41159-4

60 59 58 57 56 55 54 53 52 51 50   14 15 16/0

Printed in the U.S.A.   40

CONTENTS

Author's Note

Some biographies and reference books give Amelia Earhart's birth date as July 24, 1897, while others give it as July 24, 1898. In this book I have used 1897, the year given on her birth and baptismal certificates and also the year in which the announcement of her birth appeared in the Atchison newspaper, *The Globe.*

FLIGHT INTO YESTERDAY

It was midmorning, July 2, 1937, when the two fliers climbed aboard their plane at Lae, New Guinea. The tropical sun blazed in a blue sky, and the plane glittered as it taxied toward one end of the airfield. Its pilot was Amelia Earhart, whose daring flights had made her famous. With her navigator Fred Noonan, she was attempting what had never been done before: a flight around the world at the equator. So far they had flown 22,000 miles in less than a month. Now they were starting the final legs of the trip.

The plane reached the end of the runway, and Amelia swung it around. Home was 7,000 miles away, on the far side of the Pacific Ocean, and she yearned to be there. But one thing at a time. At this moment her job was to get the plane safely off the ground. The runway stretching ahead was a strip carved out of the jungle. About 3,000 feet long, it ended at a cliff that dropped away into the ocean.

Amelia pushed both throttles forward. The plane moved slowly, heavy with fuel for the long ocean flight that lay ahead. At last it began to gather speed. It went faster and faster, hurtling toward the cliff. Almost at the very edge she felt it leave the ground. They were safely off, flying low over the ocean, but flying. Now she could concentrate on gaining altitude. She could start picking out the islands that would serve as landmarks for the early part of the flight.

Ahead she had three long ocean hops. This first one should bring them to Howland Island around dawn. From Howland they would fly on to Hawaii and from there home to Oakland, California.

The flight to Howland was, in a way, a flight into yesterday. Along the way they would cross the International Dateline, where calendars turn back a day. July 2 at Lae was still July 1 at Howland, on the other side of the dateline.

This leg was also the most dangerous of the entire trip. Howland, 2,600 miles to the east, was a tiny speck of land in the middle of the vast Pacific. It would take all of her skill as a pilot and Fred's as a navigator to find the island. But danger did not worry her. She knew that flying carried risks. She faced them and accepted them.

What mattered was setting herself a challenge and meeting it. What mattered was showing that women could do what men could do and encouraging other women to do what they were capable of. That was why she was flying over the Pacific, looking for a speck of land. Fame was never her goal. The important thing was to do what she had set out to do and to do it as well as she knew how.

She had been that way all her life. Amelia Earhart, world-famous flier, was very much like the young girl who once lived in Atchison, Kansas.

Amelia at age 10.

GOOD TIMES

Amelia, aged seven or eight, is running home from school. Reaching the house, she jumps the fence instead of going around by the gate. Grandmother sees her and scolds her. Proper little girls do not jump fences. For a few days Amelia uses the gate. Then she goes back to jumping the fence. Boys are allowed to jump fences. Why shouldn't girls do it, too?

Later in life, Amelia Earhart remembered her fence-jumping. It was one of many childhood memories that she wrote about. Each memory was like a photo in an album, an event or a person captured and frozen in time.

Two people turn up often in the early pages of the album of memories: Grandfather and Grandmother Otis, with whom Amelia and her younger sister, Muriel, lived for much of the time when they were children.

As a young lawyer, Grandfather Alfred Otis settled in Atchison during its early days. He set up his law practice and built a house on Quality Hill, above the Missouri River. Then he went back east to marry Amelia Harres, a member of a Philadelphia Quaker family. They traveled by train to St. Louis and by steamer down the Missouri. Atchison was then very much a frontier town. Great piles of buffalo bones lined the newly laid railroad tracks. The streets were unpaved. And Indians in blankets roamed the town, sometimes curiously fingering the cloth of Grandmother Otis's dresses or lifting the cover of her basket to see what was inside.

As time went by, Grandfather Otis prospered. He became a judge of the United States District Court and later a banker. He also made a great deal of money buying and selling land. The Otises had eight children. The fourth was Amy, the judge's favorite.

Like her mother, Amy was tall and slim, with dark hair and eyes. She was pleasant, strong-willed, a skilled horseback rider, and a good dancer. She was someone who loved books, art, and music. In 1889, the year when she had planned to go east to Vassar College, she became dangerously sick with diphtheria. She was a long time recovering and, in the end, decided against going to college. Instead, she went with her father on some of his business trips. During the summer of 1890, when the two of them were in Colorado, she became the first woman to reach the top of Pike's Peak.

Later that year, the Otises gave a ball to present Amy to society. Her brother Mark introduced her to a college friend, Edwin Stanton Earhart. Edwin was dark, handsome, and charming, and he was a law student at the University of Kansas at Lawrence. Years later Amy told her daughters, "I liked him right away, and I soon knew he liked me, too."

Edwin was the twelfth and youngest child of the Reverend David Earhart, an Evangelical Lutheran minister, and his wife Mary. The Earharts had arrived in Atchison from Pennsylvania in 1860, about the same time as the Otises. Rev. Earhart rode as much as fifty miles each Sunday to visit his small and scattered congregations of pioneers and Indians. Weekdays he taught Greek and Hebrew at a small Lutheran college and also tried to scratch a living from the soil, fighting droughts, dust storms, crop failures, and plagues of grasshoppers. His greatest hope was that Edwin, too, would become a minister. But Edwin chose law and worked his way through the university by tutoring, tending furnaces, and shining shoes.

Edwin was not what Judge Otis had had in mind as a husband for Amy. He might have been intel-

Amy Otis and Edwin Earhart on their wedding day.

ligent, talented, and a lover of books and music, but as the judge saw him, he was too easygoing, a dreamer of big dreams rather than a doer of deeds. He refused to let them marry until Edwin was earning at least fifty dollars a month. It took Edwin five years to reach that goal, but Amy waited. After a small wedding they moved into a house the judge had bought for them in Kansas City, Kansas.

Their first daughter was born in Atchison, in the Otis house, on July 24, 1897. She was named Amelia Mary, after her two grandmothers. Three years later their second daughter, Muriel, was born.

In the family, Amelia was known as Meely. Muriel was called Pidge, after the blue pigeon in her favorite song.

Edwin's work was mostly as a claims agent for railroads. If, for example, a train derailed and the freight was damaged, Edwin dealt with the shipper. He was paid a fee for each claim he settled. It was work that took him away from home a lot. Amy often went with him on the longer trips, and so Meely and Pidge spent the school year with their Otis grandparents — their Earhart grandparents had died by then. They returned to their parents for the summer. The two girls did not mind this way of life at all. They had each other for company, and they had a warm and loving family wherever they were. Looking back much later, Amelia remembered them as wonderful years. With cousins, friends, and her sister, she had mudfights and picnics, explored caves in the bluff, and searched for arrowheads.

Amelia was slim, active, and athletic, a tomboy who never played with dolls. All through her childhood, she liked the sports and games and books meant for boys and did not see why girls should not enjoy them, too.

She was lucky to have parents who let her be the kind of person she needed to be. If she and Pidge wanted footballs for Christmas, they were given footballs. Their father took them fishing. One night, she remembered, he let them stay up late to see an eclipse of the moon. Their mother would call them to see how an earthworm was able to move without legs. While cutting up a chicken, she showed them how the lungs fitted in the body and how the wings were jointed, as cur hands and wrists are. From time to time the parents took the girls out of school to go on one of their father's business trips. They felt that anything unusual was educational.

Once, though, Amy Earhart's ideas were too advanced even for Meely. That was when Amy made the girls bloomers, or gym suits: dark blue flannel knickers, full and pleated, and gathered in at the knee. Bloomers had been invented by Amelia Jenks Bloomer, a leader in the struggle to win voting rights for women. She had thought of bloomers as a way to free women from the long skirts that they wore in her day. Amy Earhart thought her active daughters would enjoy them. As a grown-up, Amelia remembered them clearly. She had felt wonderfully free and athletic wearing bloomers. But she also felt more different from other girls than she truly liked.

In later life, people used to ask Amelia if she had been mechanical as a child. She would smile and say she guessed she had been, thinking of the chicken trap she had invented at age six. A neighbor in Kansas City kept chickens that were always escaping and invading the Earhart garden. Meely made a trap out of an orange crate with a hinged

10

*Meely on stilts and Pidge on the swing. They are
wearing the bloomers their mother made.*

lid. The lid was propped up with a stick. One end of a long string was attached to the stick. Meely, hidden behind a tree, held the other end. When she pulled, the stick flew out and the lid slammed shut. One day a chicken followed the trail of breadcrumbs that led into the trap. Meely pulled the string, and the chicken was trapped in the crate, squawking and flapping its wings. Both terrified and delighted by what she had done, Meely raced into the house. What, she asked her mother, should she do now? "Why, give it back," her mother said. "I'm sure you understand that keeping it would be stealing."

"What a blow!" Amelia later wrote.

Then, too, there was the roller coaster she built. Edwin had been paid a large bonus and he spent it to take his family to a big fair in St. Louis, the Louisiana Purchase Exposition. Meely was greatly impressed by the roller coaster. Back in Atchison, she set about building one. With old planks, Meely and her cousins built a track from the woodshed roof to the ground. Boards and roller skates became the car. The first passenger was Meely. The car swooped down the track, hit the ground, and flipped over. Meely dusted herself off and studied the problem. What they needed was a longer track, she decided. The track was made longer and she swooshed down again, this time safely. But once her grandparents saw it, the roller coaster did not last long. It was too dangerous.

The sled was another sharp memory. First there was the delight of opening a mysterious, big, flat package at Christmas and finding inside the kind of sled that boys had. A girl's sled at that time was like a little chair on wooden runners. The rider sat upright against the back of the sled and coasted down the hill. Edwin Earhart had bought his daughters flat sleds with steel runners, the kind they could use for taking belly whoppers.

Amelia never forgot the time when her sled saved her from a serious accident. She was zipping down a steep hill, when a junkman's cart pulled out of a side street into her path. The junkman did not see or hear her. The horse wore blinders and did not see her as it picked its way along. The hill was so icy that Meely could neither stop nor turn. So she coasted straight on and steered between the front and rear legs of the horse. If she had been sitting up, her head would have slammed against the horse's side.

A favorite game was called bogie and was played in an old carriage in the barn behind the Atchison house. Meely, Pidge, and their cousins took imaginary journeys behind teams of galloping horses. They had hair-raising adventures as they lost their way, bogged down in swamps, or were attacked by wolves. In the carriage they traveled far and wide. Years later, flying over Africa, Amelia thought back to trips in the carriage when they explored Africa,

13

A family picture, taken around 1907, in back of the Otis house, in Atchison, where Meely and Pidge spent their early school years. From left to right: Pidge, Uncle Carl Otis, Grandmother Otis, Meely, Uncle Carl's wife, Amy and Edwin Earhart.

taking special pleasure in the place names — Senegal, Timbuktu, Ngami, Khartoum.

On warm Saturdays they used to cook lunch outdoors, using a brick fireplace they had built themselves. The main dish they made was fried eggs. Meely was never really interested in cooking, except as a way of carrying out experiments. She felt, for example, that husking corn and shelling peas were a waste of time, energy, and food. Surely it would be better to eat the pods and the husks along with the peas and the corn. Finally, she was given permission to carry out her experiment. It clearly showed that peas were better shelled and that perhaps people were not meant to eat corn husks.

Books were always part of her childhood memories. The whole family loved to read, either aloud to others or to themselves. In Atchison, there was a large library in the judge's house. Meely spent hours reading the novels of Scott and Dickens, as well as bound volumes of magazines for young people and children's books. She wondered, both as a child and as a grown-up, why the girls in books were never allowed to have the exciting adventures that boys did. It did not seem fair, either to the girls in the stories or to the girl readers.

Meely also loved horses. She climbed onto delivery horses in front of the house. She became friends with two girls whose father had a butcher shop and who let her ride the horse that drew his wagon. She and Pidge read and reread *Black Beauty*. The sufferings of Beauty and Ginger filled them with anger against cruel adults. Their hearts ached for the tired horses whipped up and down the streets by delivery boys. Sometimes, when no one was looking, they undid a checkrein, the strap used to keep a horse from lowering its head.

They befriended a mare belonging to a neighbor who treated her cruelly. One day the mare bolted to escape the whip, ran away, and plunged over a bridge to her death, an event Amelia never forgot. The owner had been slightly injured in the chase, and Amy Earhart asked Amelia to take him a piece of cake. But Meely, who never disobeyed her mother, this time put her hands behind her back and silently shook her head. She could not, would not, take cake to a man who had been so cruel to his horse.

One lovely June day, Meely and Pidge, wearing their best dresses, were heading for Prize Day at school. Meely had worked long and hard memorizing the poem she was to recite. Along the way they stopped to see a horse they were sometimes allowed to ride. Meely discovered that through an oversight the horse had not been watered or fed since the night before. There was no question in her mind of what she should do. She set about watering and feeding the horse and putting clean straw in his stall. As she was finishing, she heard the town clock strike two. The school program was nearly over. Amelia raced to school and arrived just as the poetry contest ended. But, she told her favorite teacher later, she didn't mind. She was glad to know the poem and had had fun learning it. That was what counted, not the prize.

The memories of Atchison and Kansas City were of happy, carefree days. But change was on the way. It began when Edwin was offered a job with a salary in the claims department of the Rock Island Railroad. He accepted the job because it would mean a steady, reliable income for his family. It meant comfort and security for the first time in his marriage. In 1907 Amy and Edwin Earhart moved to Des Moines, Iowa. Meely and Pidge spent one last year with their grandparents while their mother hunted for a suitable house. In 1908 they left Atchison to live full time with their parents.

HARD TIMES

At first, life in Des Moines went well for the Earharts. They were happy to be together. They had a nice house, and money was no longer a constant worry.

The girls had vegetable gardens in the backyard, and their mother promised to buy what they raised. Pidge worked hard, but Meely decided to experiment. She wanted to see whether the weeds or the vegetables would win out. She also said she was growing a new vegetable. It turned out to be radishes the size of potatoes with two-foot-high tops, which she called Ear-dish. But even boiled, buttered, and salted, Ear-dish seemed, like the corn husks, not to be something people were meant to eat.

To celebrate Amelia's birthday that summer, Edwin took his family to the Iowa State Fair. There were pony rides and a merry-go-round and lots of interesting things to see and do. Among the things to see was an airplane that was on display and was going to fly. That was what Edwin wanted to see. Like most other people, he had never seen an airplane, but he had wanted to ever since reading about the Wright brothers' flight at Kitty Hawk a few years earlier. He persuaded the girls to come with him.

It was also Amelia's first sight of an airplane, but she was not impressed. She remembered years later looking briefly at a thing made of wood and rusty wire. She was much more interested in a funny hat made of a peach basket that she had just bought for fifteen cents.

That summer, for the first time in his life, Edwin Earhart was able to take a vacation. The family went to Worthington, Minnesota, for the month of August. They stayed at the postmaster's house and ate their meals at a boarding house. Good memories piled up. The girls rode a pony, played tennis, swam in the lake, went fishing, helped milk cows, and went on picnics. The whole family had its first ride in an automobile.

Back in Des Moines there were concerts and art exhibits, and of course books. If the girls had housework to do, one read aloud while the other did the chores. Their father often read to the family after dinner. He also had a talent for making up

19

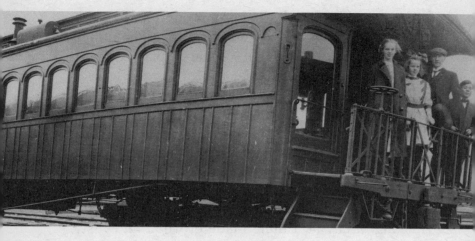

Edwin sometimes took his family with him on business trips. In this photograph, Amelia, Muriel, and Edwin are standing on the platform of their private car, with their Japanese cook.

stories, usually thrilling westerns, with himself as hero. They were stories that continued night after night and were likely to spill over into Saturday afternoons outdoors. When Edwin came home from his morning at the office, he would play cowboys and pioneers with the girls and their friends.

Edwin was doing well. He was promoted to head of the claims department, and his salary almost doubled. The family moved to an even nicer house. Edwin still traveled a great deal for the railroad, sometimes in a private car. He took his family as far as California.

Then the bad times began. They began because Edwin had started to drink and was soon drinking more than he could handle. The good memories changed to ones of misery.

It was Saturday afternoon. The girls and their friends were playing outdoors when they saw Edwin getting off the streetcar a block away. They ran shouting to meet him, but were puzzled by the way he was walking. He seemed unsteady and was putting each foot down with great care. "Can't play today," he said and went into the house.

The next morning before church Amy Earhart spoke to the girls. She explained that every now and then some of the men in their father's office asked him to have a drink with them. He accepted so as not to seem rude. Edwin himself was sorry for what had happened on Saturday and promised it would never happen again.

His good intentions did not last. Soon he was having a few drinks, then far too many.

Family life changed. Meely and Pidge would listen for their father's footsteps outside the house. Brisk steps meant the father they knew and loved was coming home. Shuffling steps meant the thick-tongued stranger, who was often in bad temper. They soon learned never to joke at the dinner table, because whatever they said was cause for anger. They ate as quickly and quietly as possible, eager to get away from the table. They felt deserted, unloved, and unhappy. Yet, at the same time, they were too loyal and proud ever to say a word to friends about what was happening at home.

Edwin's work was suffering. He failed to show up for business dates and failed to handle paperwork. Word of his drinking reached the head office in Chicago. He was warned to keep away from "the drinking crowd," but he didn't. Finally, Edwin agreed to go to a hospital for a month's cure.

He returned in fine shape to a warm welcome. Amy had bought him a carpenter's bench in hopes that he would enjoy a hobby. Meely and Pidge had picked cherries for a neighbor and earned enough money to buy him a new fishing rod. But he was soon drinking again and this time lost his job.

A new job was hard to find. Edwin was both intelligent and able, but no one wanted to hire a man who couldn't be trusted to stay sober. At last he found a job as a clerk in the freight office of the Great Northern Railway in St. Paul, Minnesota. The family packed up and moved.

In St. Paul, Edwin continued to drink. The strain was showing in Amy's health; and for the girls, he continued to be a father they could not rely on.

There was a Twelfth Night dance at St. Clement's, the Episcopal church the family attended. Two boys had urged Amelia and Muriel to come to the dance, and they were looking forward to it. In those days girls were taken to parties by their fathers and called for by their fathers, unless a neighborhood group was to come home together. Edwin had promised to be home in time to change his clothes and take them to the party. He would stay long enough to dance one dance with each of them, since they were not sure anyone would ask them to dance right away. They were to come home with friends, and Amy had arranged refreshments for the group.

Eight o'clock, the time of the party, came and went. About nine Edwin arrived home. One glance told them he could not possibly escort them to the dance. Muriel rushed upstairs and cried. Amelia went silently into the living room, took down the decorations, and put away the food.

Nothing seemed to work out. A few months later, Edwin staggered into the path of an automobile, was slightly injured, and spent a few days in the hospital.

Then he was offered a job in the claims office of the Burlington Railroad in Springfield, Missouri. He was delighted by the chance to do legal work again and accepted the job. Once more the family packed and moved on, leaving behind the friends they had just started to make.

They arrived in Springfield and immediately discovered that there was no job. It was all a misunderstanding. The employee that Edwin was to replace had decided not to retire after all.

Fortunately, Amy Earhart had a small income,

which had come to her after her parents' death. Otherwise the family would have had no money at all. Even so, it seemed that the time had come to separate, at least for a while. Amy and her daughters went to stay with friends in Chicago. Edwin went back to Kansas City, where he opened a law office and lived with one of his sisters and her family.

Amelia wanted to get through school on schedule. She liked English and languages, but was most interested in science, especially physics and chemistry. After looking at several high schools, she chose to enter Hyde Park, which seemed to offer the best science courses. She was determined to make good, and she worked hard.

Her English class, however, had a teacher who was almost totally deaf. The students took advantage of the teacher's deafness. When the teacher read aloud, they chattered. When she asked questions, they amused themselves by reciting "Mary Had a Little Lamb" instead of answering. Amelia felt class time was wasted and that it was cruel to make fun of a helpless old person. She got up a petition asking to be assigned another teacher. At the last moment, the other students refused to sign and tore up the petition. After that, Amelia managed to spend the English period reading in the school library. She received class credits for reading four times as many books as required, but she was avoided by her classmates. The caption under her picture in the class of 1916 read: "The girl in brown, who walks alone." It hurt.

Amelia did not go to graduation. The important thing was doing her best, passing her courses, and graduating. She didn't care about a piece of paper saying she had done so.

That summer the family was reunited in Kansas City. Edwin had stopped drinking and was practicing law again, working for himself, which was what he liked best. He had found a small house, where they could be together, but his years of drinking had left their mark on the family. There was no going back to the way things used to be.

As an adult, Amelia never drank alcohol. And she never spoke or wrote about her father's drinking and the pain it caused. Through it all, she had never ceased to love him deeply and to remember the wonderful father he had been when she was a child.

The bad years also taught her an important lesson about setting goals and reaching them. She had been determined not to fall behind in school, in spite of all the moves and her own unhappiness. She had worked hard, and she had reached her goal. In doing it, she may also have decided that in the future she would go her own way and depend only on herself.

But in the summer of 1916, it was not yet clear what that way would be.

WHAT NEXT?

Amelia was young, bright, and full of energy and curiosity. But she didn't know what she wanted to do with herself. For a time she attended the Ogontz School, near Philadelphia, with the idea of going on to Bryn Mawr College. While at Ogontz she kept a scrapbook of clippings from newspapers and magazines. Each article told of a woman who had made a career for herself. There was a fire lookout, a bank president, a brick layer, a president of a medical association, and many others with jobs that were once held only by men.

In December 1917 she went to Canada and spent Christmas with Muriel, who was in school in Toronto. At that time the United States had not yet entered World War I, but Canadians had been

Amelia became a nurse's aide in a Toronto hospital for veterans.

fighting for more than three years. In Toronto she realized for the first time that war was more than brass bands and shiny buttons on new uniforms. It was also men without arms and legs, men who were blind or paralyzed. One day she saw four one-legged men swinging down a sidewalk on crutches together. Somehow she had to help. She dropped out of school and volunteered as a nurse's aide in a Toronto hospital for veterans. She stayed there until the armistice in November 1918, working ten hours a day.

When there was time, Amelia and Muriel went

horseback riding with officers of the nearby Canadian Flying School. Sometimes they were invited to watch the officers fly. Civilians were not allowed to go up in the planes, but Amelia enjoyed spending time at the field and learning all she could. She loved the sting of snow on her face, blown by propellers as the training planes took off.

One day she went with a friend to see an exhibition of stunt flying by aces returned from the war. The two watched from the middle of a clearing as a little plane looped and rolled and spun in the air. Then the pilot, having no more stunts to perform, began to amuse himself by diving at the crowd and watching it scatter. Seeing two young women he began to dive at them. The friend ran, but Amelia stood her ground and felt a strange mixture of fear and pleasure as the plane swooped low and the red wings swooshed by her. But she still did not think of flying herself. There was no reason to. Flying was simply a sport for those who knew how to do it.

Amelia left Toronto and spent some time in Northampton, Massachusetts, where Muriel was preparing to enter Smith College. While she was there, she bought a banjo and took lessons and also took a course in automobile engine repair.

Her next stop was New York City, where she entered Columbia University. She had liked working in the hospital and was thinking about a career in medicine. But she soon found that she didn't want to be a doctor, although she liked her science courses and the experiments. She thought she might work in medical research. But her parents, who had moved to Los Angeles, were asking her to come home. She left Columbia to see if she could help them stay together.

The Earharts were living in a large house with extra rooms that they rented out. One of the boarders was a young man named Sam Chapman, a chemical engineer. He was attracted to Amelia, who was tall and slim, straightforward in manner, with a cheerful grin and level gray eyes. She also had a wry sense

Sam Chapman and Amelia shared many interests, among them a love of the outdoors.

of humor. They both enjoyed tennis and swimming, books and plays. Amelia liked Sam, liked being with him, but she was not interested in marrying and settling down. She had gone to California thinking that she might continue her medical studies. But before she even started something else caught her attention.

A number of wartime fliers were trying to earn a living with planes. They gave lessons, and they put on air circuses, doing stunts in their planes. Amelia started attending air circuses. Often she took her father along and got him to ask questions of the pilots. She learned that most people learned to fly in about ten hours and that the necessary lessons would cost five hundred dollars.

Her father arranged a trial flight for her. Amelia went to the airfield, which was an open space on Wilshire Boulevard, and climbed aboard the plane. They took off. The ocean came into view, miles away. The Hollywood hills seemed just outside the cockpit. Now she knew. More than anything else she wanted to fly.

She signed up for lessons, then learned that her father could not pay for them. So she set about earning the money herself. She went out and found her first job, in the mail room of the telephone company.

Whenever she was free, Amelia rode the streetcar to the end of the line, got off, and walked several miles along a dusty road to the airfield. In her lessons she learned takeoffs, landings, slips, stalls, spins, and loops. She was not learning stunts, but what to do if her plane stalled or went into a spin accidentally. Much of the time she just hung around, watching and listening. She was not earning enough money to pay for many lessons.

Soon she was dressing like the other fliers, for the field was dusty, and the planes awkward to climb into. She wore boots and khaki pants, a scarf around her neck, a knee-length flying jacket, a helmet with goggles to protect her eyes in the open cockpit. She had also had her hair cut short. When she first bought her jacket, she slept in it for a few nights to give it a used look.

In 1921 she soloed, going up to 5,000 feet, doing what she had to do, and landing. Most students making their first solo put off having to land until they had no choice — until they were almost out of gas. Amelia did not. When she was ready, she flew back and landed.

By the next summer she had her own plane. The Otis house on Quality Hill had been sold and some of the money went to Amy Earhart. She helped Amelia buy a small, second-hand plane, a Kinner Canary, which had a speed of seventy miles per hour at 5,000 feet. The little yellow plane had been built by a local man. It was the only one he had, so he and Amelia arranged to share it. He gave her

Amelia's first instructor was Neta Snook (left), one of the first women to earn a pilot's license in the United States.

free hangar space. In return, she let him use the plane as a demonstrator with people who might want to order one.

Between working at various jobs, Amelia flew as much as she could. A few other American women were flying and setting records. Amelia decided to try her hand at it. She soared to 14,000 feet before her engine stalled, setting a new altitude record for women. The record stood for a few weeks, then was broken by another woman pilot, Ruth Nichols. Amelia also had her share of accidents. Once a rainstorm forced her to crash-land in a farmer's field. The plane nosed over, and Amelia hung upside down from her safety belt. Another time when she was forced down and the plane nosed over, her safety belt broke and she fell from the cockpit. But both times she walked away unhurt. She accepted accidents as part of flying. In the early 1920s all pilots expected to make emergency landings because of engine failure.

By the summer of 1924 Edwin and Amy Earhart had agreed to a divorce. Amy and her daughters decided to return to the East Coast. Amelia sold her plane and bought a canary yellow touring car, a Kissel, for the trip. She was still not sure what she wanted to do with her life. She flew only for fun, and although she loved it more than anything else, flying did not seem to offer much hope of a career.

Amelia returned to New York City and Columbia, where she took physics and other courses that interested her. That summer she went to Boston, where Muriel was teaching. After trying various jobs, she finally found one that she liked. She became a social worker at Denison House, Boston's second oldest settlement house. There she worked with foreigners, mostly Syrian and Chinese, who had recently emigrated to the United States. There were games and classes for children after school. Mothers and fathers learned how to read and write English. There were plays to be put on, story-telling hours, and classes in cooking and sewing. It was the first job she had truly enjoyed, and she felt she was learning as much as she was teaching. She had never before had a chance to learn about people from other lands.

What started as a part-time job soon became full time, and she lived at Denison House. She had little free time, but she flew when she could. She joined an aviation association. And with Ruth Nichols of Rye, New York, she was trying to work out a way of organizing women in aviation. There was also Sam Chapman, who had followed Amelia east. He was trying to persuade her to give up social work and marry him. But she knew it would not work. He could not accept a working wife, and she could not give up her independence. Amelia turned him down, but they remained good friends.

Then, one April day in 1928, when she was busy at Denison House, she received a phone call from a man she had never heard of. It was a call that changed her life forever. Because of it, she became the first woman to cross the Atlantic Ocean by air.

THE ROAD TO FAME

The 1920s were an exciting time in the young world of aviation. Daring fliers were crossing oceans and making trips that had never before been possible. Record flight after record flight made headlines in newspapers. The fliers were heroes, and everyone wanted to see them and read about them.

On May 20, 1927, a young man named Charles Lindbergh took off from Long Island, New York, and made the first nonstop solo flight across the Atlantic. He arrived in Paris, France, on May 21, thirty-three and a half hours after takeoff, becoming famous overnight.

So far, only men had played a part in these record-breaking flights. But that was about to change. In London, England, a wealthy woman, Amy Phipps

While working in Boston, Amelia had little free time, but she flew whenever she could.

Guest, decided it was time for a woman to cross the Atlantic by air. She wanted to be that woman. Without telling of her plan, Mrs. Guest quietly bought a plane. It was the trimotor Fokker that Commander Richard E. Byrd of the United States had used on a recent flight around the North Pole. Mrs. Guest named the plane *Friendship*. She saw the flight as a symbol of good will between the United States, where she had been born, and England, where she now lived.

As things turned out, Mrs. Guest's family persuaded her not to make the flight herself. But she still wanted an American to be the first woman to cross the Atlantic by air.

Because she was keeping in touch with fliers and flying, Amelia Earhart soon came to the attention of the men who were to find a substitute for Mrs. Guest. She was interviewed in Boston and then again in New York. One of the men who talked with her in New York was George Palmer Putnam, who had published Lindbergh's book about his transatlantic flight. Amelia was asked a lot of questions. She also learned that the pilot and mechanic for the flight would be paid. The American woman would not. Her reward would be the adventure and the opportunities that might open up for her in aviation and in writing.

Amelia went back to Boston hoping she had made the right impression. If the interviewers had not found her attractive, she would never be chosen as the symbol of good will. On the other hand, if they found her too attractive, they might not be willing to risk drowning her. She hoped she had come out somewhere in the middle.

There was never any real question in the minds of the interviewers. She was the right choice — and as a bonus, the men noticed, she looked enough like Charles Lindbergh to be his sister.

Much work lay ahead in preparing for the flight. What they were doing was kept secret. They did not want to talk about the flight until it was a fact.

Amelia was captain of the flight. She would be in charge and make all decisions, but she lacked the necessary experience to do the flying herself.

The pilot was Bill Stultz, a young man who was a highly skilled pilot, navigator, and radio operator. He was known to be a problem drinker, but Amelia was told Bill was always all right once he had his hands on the controls. The mechanic was Slim Gordon. Like Bill, he had learned his skills in the U.S. Army.

The *Friendship* had been a land plane with wheels. For the Atlantic crossing, it was fitted with pontoons and changed into a seaplane. It had three Wright Whirlwind engines of 225 horsepower each. Two gasoline tanks were built into the cabin. With those and the tanks in the wings, the plane could carry 900 gallons of fuel. The wings were painted gold. The body, or fuselage, was a bright orange, which would make the plane easier to spot if it came down at sea.

While preparations were being made, Amelia went on working at Denison House. She had not told her parents what she was about to do; she knew it was dangerous. So she wrote each of them a note, to be opened only if the *Friendship* crashed. To her mother she said, "My life has really been very happy and I didn't mind contemplating its end in the midst of it." To her father she said, "Hooray for the last grand adventure! I wish I had won but it was worth while anyway."

In late May they were ready. Two attempts to get away from Boston failed because the weather was against them. When they finally were able to take off, they headed straight up the coast and ran into thick fog. Since there were no instruments for flying blind at that time, they looked for a hole in the fog and landed at Halifax, Nova Scotia.

The next day was beautifully clear, with just the right wind. They flew to Trepassey, Newfoundland, their starting point for the Atlantic flight, and landed to take on fuel. But weather and mechanical difficulties trapped them for thirteen long days. Strong winds churned the bay, making takeoff impossible. A pontoon sprung a leak and an oil tank cracked. Slim repaired them. The fliers passed their time playing rummy, chopping wood, studying maps and weather reports, hiking, and fishing. Under strain, Bill began drinking heavily, but Slim thought he would be all right once they were in the air.

On June 12 they tried for the second time to take off. The plane felt heavy. They got rid of cameras, coats, bags, everything they could spare. They still could not take off. The next day they unloaded 200 gallons of fuel. This lessened both their margin of safety and their cruising range. With only 700 gallons of gasoline they could at best reach Ireland. But even with the lighter load they still could not get off.

Amelia had a decision to make. There was a backup pilot waiting in Boston in case he was needed. Should she send for him? She was tempted to. But if she did, she would hurt Bill and greatly harm his career. She might even endanger the whole project. In the end, she decided to stay with Bill and hope that the weather would take a turn for the better before he cracked up.

Finally, in late morning of June 17, 1928, the wind was in the right direction, and the weather forecast seemed promising. Amelia and Slim got Bill out of bed and helped him aboard the plane.

Three times Bill taxied into position, facing the wind. Three times the plane charged down the bay but could not get up enough speed to take off. They tried a fourth time. As before, Amelia was crouched in the cabin with a stop watch in hand to check the take-off time. Her eyes were fixed on the speed indicator. They would have to reach a speed of at least fifty-five miles an hour for *Friendship* to take off. Thirty . . . forty . . . fifty . . . fifty-five . . . sixty — they were off at last.

With two engines sputtering from salt spray, they climbed to 3,000 feet and ran into fog. They climbed higher and met a snowstorm. Bill headed down and they broke into clear skies and sunshine, with a blue sea below them. It didn't last. They were soon either flying through clouds or above them. Amelia was entranced by what she was seeing — the shapes of the clouds, the pink tint added by the setting sun, the gray hollows and shadows. She later wrote that she had spent her time kneeling at the window "gulping beauty."

In the north, summer nights are short, and they were flying east, toward the sun. They flew through only five hours of darkness. But even in daylight fog kept them from seeing the ocean, and their radio had stopped working. They could not get word from ships at sea to check their position.

About the time they thought they should be reaching Ireland, Bill dropped down through the clouds and fog. They were hoping to see land, because their gas was getting low. There was no land in sight, but they did see a big transatlantic ship. If it had left Ireland and they were headed for Ireland, plane and ship should have been on parallel courses. They weren't. The ship was cutting directly across their course. Did this mean they were lost? It was an unpleasant thought.

They circled the ship, hoping the captain would guess what they wanted and have the ship's position painted on the deck so that they could read it. When nothing happened, Amelia wrote their request on a piece of paper, put it in a bag weighted with two oranges, and dropped it through the hatch in the cabin floor. The message fell into the sea.

To go on circling was to waste fuel. Their choices were to ditch near the ship and be picked up or to go on. They chose to go on. It was the right decision. Soon they saw two small fishing boats, a sign that land was near, then another transatlantic ship. As it turned out, they had passed Ireland and were now approaching Wales. They saw a little town and decided to land there. Bill set the *Friendship* down in the harbor and taxied to a buoy, where they tied up.

Thanks to the skill of Bill Stultz, they had arrived safely, after a flight of twenty hours, forty minutes, and for the first time a woman had crossed the Atlantic by air. But because the plane's radio was not working, there was no way they could send out word of their achievement.

On shore, no one paid much attention to them. Three men who were working on the railroad came to the water's edge, looked at the plane, and then went back to work. After a while, people from the village came down and looked at the plane. Slim Gordon climbed out onto a pontoon and called for a boat. Nothing happened. Amelia waved a white towel to signal for help. One of the men on shore took off his coat and, in a friendly fashion, used it to wave back.

Finally, boats came out to the plane, *Friendship* was moored for the night, and the weary crew went ashore. They found themselves in Burry Port, and as word spread of who they were, thousands of Welsh turned out to greet them. The next day they

Amelia looks out the door of Friendship *at its mooring in Southhampton harbor.*

flew to Southampton, England, where they were met by Mrs. Guest, the press, and crowds of people eager to see the first woman to cross the Atlantic by air.

The next two weeks were a jumble of teas, dinners, tennis and polo matches, sightseeing, and a visit to Parliament. Everywhere the fliers went, Amelia was the center of attention. After they returned home by ship, there were parades, receptions, medals in New York, Boston, and Chicago. Through it all, Amelia was the flier that everyone wanted to see, interview, and photograph. She was bothered by her fame, feeling that she had only been a passenger on the flight. Bill Stultz and Slim Gordon were the ones who had made the flight a success. They deserved the credit and attention that she was getting. But there was nothing she could do except try her best to fill the role she found herself in. For the sake of her self-respect, she made a silent promise: Someday she would fly the Atlantic herself.

Meanwhile, George Putnam was acting as Amelia's manager, dealing with requests for magazine articles and lectures. He was also to be the publisher of her book *20 Hrs., 40 Min.,* an account of the flight. At his suggestion, she stayed with him and his wife in Rye, New York, while she was writing it. When she finished, she felt a deep need to get away from people and be by herself. It was time to get back in the air.

BUSY YEARS

While in England, Amelia had flown, liked, and bought a small airplane. It was the Avro Moth that Lady Mary Heath had flown from Capetown, South Africa, to London. The wings could be folded up and the plane was so light that Amelia could move it by picking up the tail and pulling. The plane arrived by ship just as she was finishing her book.

Amelia bought some road maps, which were what fliers used in 1928, and headed for California. She found her way by following roads, railroad tracks, and rivers and by picking out towns as they appeared on a map. The map was pinned to her clothes to keep it from blowing out of the open cockpit.

The trip was going well. She felt splendidly free, flying alone and landing for the night wherever she pleased. Then, after leaving Fort Worth, Texas, she lost her map. A gust of wind seized it, tore it loose from the pin, and blew it away. This part of Texas had wide plains and an empty horizon. It offered few clues to where she was or where she was heading. Amelia found a highway and decided to follow the cars on it, feeling that they must be going somewhere. But one by one they turned off and disappeared. Daylight was fading, gas was running low, and she seemed to be in the middle of nowhere. Finally she spotted a very small town and landed on its main street. The townspeople welcomed her and put her up for the night.

The next morning Amelia followed a railroad to Pecos. She was heading for El Paso in the afternoon when engine trouble forced her to land among the mesquite bushes. Luckily, she was near a road. Cars stopped, help came, and she was soon on her way again.

In the fall of 1928 Amelia flew back to the East Coast. She discovered that without knowing it she had become the first woman to fly from the Atlantic to the Pacific and back again. She discovered too that during her absence offers had been pouring in from people who wanted to hire her to lecture or write. George Putnam had been lining up lecture dates for her. She joined the staff of *Cosmopolitan* magazine and wrote an article nearly every month: "Try Flying Yourself," "Is It Safe to Fly?" "Why

Are Women Afraid to Fly?" But writing about flying was not the same as flying. She learned that the first Women's Air Derby would be held in August of 1929. Amelia decided to enter. She sold her Moth and bought a Lockheed Vega, a more powerful plane that could make longer, faster flights.

Twenty fliers set out on August 18, 1929. Their course led from Santa Monica, California, to Cleveland, Ohio. The race was to take eight days, with many stops along the way and no night flying. Even so, there were accidents and dropouts. At Yuma, Arizona, Amelia ran into a sandbank while landing and cracked her propeller. The accident could have cost her the race, but the other fliers voted to stay at Yuma until repairs were made.

On the seventh day the fliers arrived at Columbus, Ohio. Two pilots were tied for first place. One was Amelia, or AE, as she liked to be known, having never been fond of her given name. The other was Ruth Nichols. Each would be trying to make the best time on the last hop to Cleveland. Ruth Nichols was to take off just before AE, but she crashed. One wing dipped, then the plane hit a tractor at the end of the runway and flipped over. Instead of taking off, AE jumped to the ground, ran to the wrecked plane, and pulled her friend out. Only when she was sure that Ruth was uninjured did Amelia take off for Cleveland. Because of the lost time, she finished third.

That fall Amelia lectured and wrote. What she liked best about earning money was that she could use it to help other people. Her father, who had remarried, was suffering from cancer of the throat. She paid his medical bills, and to ease his mind, paid off the mortgage on his house. After he died in 1930 she paid his debts. Throughout her life, she helped her mother, sister, friends, and Denison House.

New opportunities arose, because aviation was changing. For some years fliers had been showing the world what human beings could do in airplanes. There were altitude records and speed records to be set. There were flights to be made that had never been made before. Now flying was starting to be recognized as a form of transportation. Pilots were proving that airplanes could deliver passengers and mail safely and on schedule.

AE joined one of the pioneer passenger airlines. Her job was to sell flying to women, both by lecturing and making sure that passengers were satisfied. She flew all over the country and often took her mother with her. She helped to start a new airline that offered hourly service between New York City and Washington, D.C. But her heart was not in business, even the airline business. She was eager to get back to flying and did.

She set new speed records for women over one-mile and one-hundred-kilometer courses. She learned to fly an autogiro, an early kind of helicopter, and set an altitude record of 18,415 feet. Later she flew an autogiro from the East Coast to Oakland, California.

And in 1930 she decided to marry George Palmer Putnam, who was now divorced. GP, as he was often called, was intelligent, handsome, educated, successful at whatever he tried, and a man of action. Since the first Atlantic flight, he had been managing and promoting Amelia's career, making himself part of her life. He wanted to marry Amelia and proposed several times. But Amelia was wary of marriage,

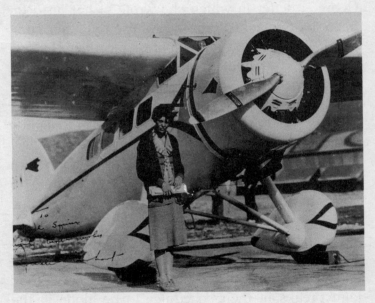

AE and her Lockheed Vega, around 1930.

which she saw as a kind of cage. She recognized in herself a deep need to be free and independent. And so she always turned George down, although they had much in common, and she enjoyed being with him.

One day they were at the Lockheed aircraft factory in Burbank, California. While Amelia waited for her plane to be warmed up, GP proposed for the sixth time. To his surprise, she nodded yes, patted his arm, and then flew off. She had apparently decided that George could be trusted not to cage her.

Even so, just before the wedding she handed George a letter in which she wrote of her need for freedom. She asked him to promise to let her go in a year if they found no happiness together. He read the letter and nodded his agreement. They were married at his mother's house in Connecticut, on February 7, 1931. Amelia, who never fussed over clothes, was bare-headed and dressed in a slightly worn brown suit and brown shoes.

GP now gave up publishing and took a job with Paramount Pictures that gave him more time to manage AE's career. He leased the use of her name for advertisements for the Franklin automobile, lightweight airplane luggage, and the kind of clothes she liked to wear herself. She wrote and lectured and flew. From time to time she and George took joint breaks in their schedules to be alone at the house in Rye or to entertain friends.

In the spring of 1932 AE made a big decision. She decided the time had come to fulfill the promise she had made herself four years earlier. She was ready to make a solo flight across the Atlantic. She was ready to prove that a woman could do what only men had done before.

FACING THE ATLANTIC

Amelia did not announce her plans ahead of time. Like many fliers, she felt that something would go wrong if she did. Also, she did not want to feel pressured. She wanted the freedom to change her mind. Only a few people knew what she was going to do.

GP, of course, knew and was full of enthusiasm. Her Lockheed Vega needed changes before she could fly it across the Atlantic. She asked an expert, Bernt Balchen, to take charge of this. He was a noted flier who had served as first pilot on Byrd's recent expedition to Antarctica. AE needed extra fuel tanks in the wings and cabin of the Vega. The fuselage had to be strengthened to support the extra weight. New navigation instruments were added, along with a 500-horsepower Pratt & Whitney engine. AE herself practiced flying blind until she felt sure she could handle the plane on instruments alone, if she had to.

When the plane was ready, all she needed was a promising weather report. It came early in the afternoon of May 19. AE didn't bother to pack. She went off in slacks, shirt, and windbreaker. She carried only a leather flying suit, a thermos of soup, and a can of tomato juice with a straw. The official takeoff point would be Harbor Grace, Newfoundland. Balchen and a mechanic went that far with her, Balchen flying so that AE could rest. They put down at St. John, New Brunswick, for the night and early the next moring flew on to Harbor Grace. AE took a nap while the plane was being fueled and Balchen gave it a final check. Then she shook hands, climbed aboard, and took off at 7:12 P.M., May 20.

The first few hours of the trip went well. The Vega was cruising at 12,000 feet in clear weather. Sunset ended and the moon rose over a low bank of clouds. Night was her favorite time to fly. She looked ahead to flying through a star-filled night and reaching Paris on the fifth anniversary of Lindbergh's arrival.

Very shortly things began to go wrong.

First the altimeter failed. Now in clouds, fog, or darkness she had no way of knowing how far above the surface of the ocean she was. She thought she could manage and flew on, instead of turning back.

Soon the moon disappeared behind clouds. The

Vega ran into a severe storm. It was tossed about by winds and air pockets and pounded by rain, as lightning crackled in the surrounding clouds. AE fought with all her strength to hold her course.

After an hour or so, she came into calmer but still cloudy weather. She glimpsed the moon and thought perhaps she could climb above the clouds. She headed up, but the plane soon became sluggish and slow to respond, a clear sign that it was picking up ice. The only thing to do was to head down into warmer air and hope the ice would melt. When she could see waves breaking on the ocean surface, she leveled off and flew on. But soon she ran into fog. Without the altimeter she could not safely fly low in fog, so she headed up again, hoping to find an altitude where the plane would neither ice up nor crash into the ocean.

Plowing through clouds and fog, she could see only one thing: A weld in her exhaust manifold had started to burn through. This was not immediately dangerous, but in time, as the crack opened up, the manifold would start to shake. It was then likely to damage the engine parts to which it was attached. Still, there was nothing to do except fly on and hope for the best.

When daylight came, AE found herself between two layers of clouds. She decided to climb into the sun's warmth, since ice was still clinging to the wings. But the glare of the sun on the tops of the

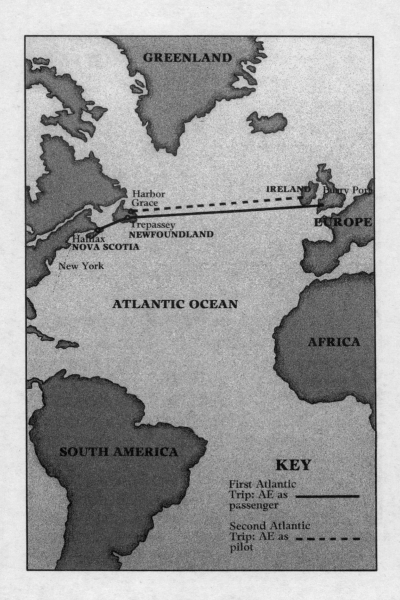

GREENLAND

IRELAND Burry Port

Harbor
Grace

Trepassey
NEWFOUNDLAND

EUROPE

Halifax
NOVA SCOTIA

New York

ATLANTIC OCEAN

AFRICA

SOUTH AMERICA

KEY

First Atlantic
Trip: AE as
passenger

Second Atlantic
Trip: AE as
pilot

When word spread of AE's arrival in Ireland, crowds of people turned out to see and greet her.

white clouds was too much for her eyes, even with dark glasses. She headed down again, flying low, hoping to see a boat.

By now the exhaust manifold was shaking badly. And when she turned on the reserve fuel tanks, she found the gauge was leaking. She gave up all hope of reaching Paris and decided to land at the first possible place. This turned out to be Ireland.

At the coast AE could see thunderstorms and hills to the south. She turned north, soon found a railroad, and followed it, hoping it would lead to a city where there might be an airport. It led to Londonderry. She did not see an airfield, but she did see meadows. After coming in low several times and, as she noted, frightening the cows, she chose her spot and landed. In spite of everything, she had done what she set out to do. She had shown that a woman could fly the Atlantic, fly it solo — and do this in fourteen hours, fifty-six minutes.

Once more AE was caught up in award ceremonies, luncheons, dinners, receptions. With GP, who had arrived by ship, she visited London, Paris, Rome, met kings and queens and presidents. When they returned home, they were guests of President and Mrs. Herbert Hoover at the White House.

Once more she was touring the country on lecture tours, writing articles, and also writing a book, *The Fun of It,* about her solo flight. Yet she was also finding time to fly and to set more records.

FIRST PACIFIC FLIGHT

Three months after she had soloed across the Atlantic, AE set a new women's speed record. She flew across the continent, from Los Angeles to New York, in nineteen hours, five minutes. Eleven months later, she flew the same course and set another record: seventeen hours, seven minutes.

She continued to lecture and write and was entertained at the White House by the new president, Franklin D. Roosevelt, and Mrs. Roosevelt. Amelia and George became friends of the Roosevelts and visited them a number of times. One night after dinner, she and Mrs. Roosevelt slipped away, borrowed a plane from Eastern Airlines, and went flying, both in evening dress. AE wanted to show Mrs. Roosevelt how beautiful night flight was.

By 1934 AE was planning a flight over 2,400

AE and Mrs. Roosevelt at a luncheon honoring AE.

miles of the Pacific, from Hawaii to California. Other
pilots had flown from California to Hawaii, but no
one had made a successful flight from west to east.
She sold her old plane and bought a new Vega, also
painted red with gold stripes down the sides. She
later wrote that it might look a little gaudy on the
ground, but must be beautiful when seen against
white clouds. She also hired an expert to help her
with navigation and technical matters. This was
Paul Mantz, a skilled pilot who often flew as a stunt
pilot in movies.

Just before Christmas, AE, GP, and Paul sailed

for Hawaii with the Vega aboard ship. Once in Hawaii AE had to wait for the right weather and also for a go-ahead from Paul, who was testing the plane and equipment.

On January 11, 1935, plane and pilot were ready, but there were rain squalls around the islands that morning. AE took a nap at noon, just in case, and at 3:30 learned that there should be good weather along her course. But she'd have to take off promptly or she might be held up another ten days by the weather that was moving in.

By 4:30 she was at Wheeler Field, where the U.S. Army had made a runway for her by mowing a path in the tall grass and staking it out with little white flags. The plane was heavy with gasoline, but she took off safely and began a slow climb. As night came on, the blue ocean became darker and darker, until it turned to black. By then the stars were out, looking as if they were close enough to touch. She was doing what she liked best — flying at night, alone with the stars.

By midmorning she was looking for land, which is always tricky if there are clouds about. Their shadows on the water look like islands and even coastlines. She was flying at 1,800 feet when she knew she had spotted the coastal hills of California. Noticing a low spot, she flew over it and saw San Francisco Bay. She crossed the bay and set the plane down in Oakland.

She was now the first person, male or female, to make the flight from Hawaii to California, first to fly solo across part of the Pacific Ocean, and first to solo over both the Atlantic and the Pacific. Ten thousand people were waiting to cheer her.

Three months later AE was off on another record-setting flight, the first person to fly solo from Los Angeles to Mexico City. She took off shortly before midnight, enjoying another night flight. By late morning, she reached Mazatlán, 1,000 miles from her starting point. Here her flight plan called for her to turn east and fly to Mexico City, arriving around 1 P.M. One o'clock came and went and there was no sign of the capital city. Where was she? To find out, she chose a dry lake bed and landed. Within minutes, men on horseback rode out from a nearby village. She did not speak Spanish and they did not speak English. But with the help of sign language and a map, she learned that she was near the village of Nopala. She took off and flew the remaining 50 miles to Mexico City.

Now her plan was to fly on across 700 miles of the Gulf of Mexico nonstop to Newark, New Jersey, setting still another new record. Bad weather delayed her for days. At last, just after midnight on May 8, she received the kind of weather bulletin she had been waiting for. She had the Vega fueled. A mechanic, working under the headlights of an automobile, gave the plane a final check. Then she was off. It was a successful flight, but it also marked a change in AE's thinking. Her ocean-crossing flights had all been made mostly at night, usually in heavy clouds and fog. She had seen little of the water. Much of her crossing of the Gulf of Mexico was made in daylight and clear weather. Looking down at nothing except water, she thought the gulf looked very large — and wet. What, she wondered, would happen if the Vega's engine conked out? She decided that she would make no more water crossings in a single-engine plane.

A little later that year, AE felt she needed a change. She needed time to think about her future. She could see that within a year or two there would be no more record-setting flights to make. Someone would have made every flight that could be made, and the period of aviation that she had loved would come to an end. She decided to accept an offer made earlier by the president of Purdue University in Indiana. She would spend part of the 1935–36 school year there, counseling women students about careers.

AE felt at home because Purdue liked to experiment with education. It even had an airfield, where students could learn to fly. She was also happy counseling the young women. She had never believed that all women should have careers. But she did believe that those who wanted careers should have the same opportunities that young men had.

*From time to time, George and Amelia managed to
spend quiet days together at their home in Rye.*

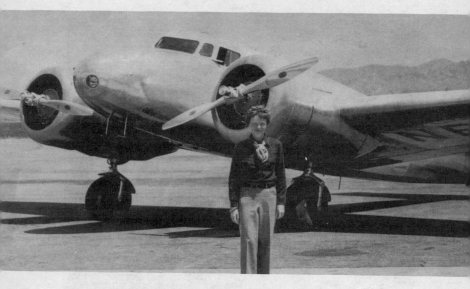

AE and her Lockheed Electra.

She did not think that comfort and security should be goals in life. She felt they kept people from being what they were truly capable of being. She believed that people should "dare to live." Over the years she had made this clear in the lectures she gave and the articles she wrote. Most of all she tried to make it clear by the way she lived her own life — by being her own person and making use of her talents. She thought it was important to be "the first woman to." She wanted to show that given a chance, women could achieve what men had achieved.

As Amelia was making plans for her future, the

Purdue Research Foundation ordered a new plane that she was to use as a flying laboratory. It was a twin-engine Lockheed Electra. She took delivery of the plane on July 24, 1936, her thirty-ninth birthday.

AE's long-range plan was to use the plane to study how flying affected people. She had many questions in mind: Does flying affect the way a person's body uses food? Is one kind of food better than another during flight? How much do the many instruments in a cockpit increase pilot fatigue? At what rate? Do men and women differ in their reactions to flight? If so, how? It was a plan that brought together her love of flying and her life-long interests in science, medicine, experimenting, and helping people.

But first there was one other thing she was going to do. She was going to face the greatest challenge left in aviation: a flight around the world at the equator. It would not be the first world flight, but all the earlier ones had been made north of the equator and made by men. If she succeeded, she would be the first woman to fly around the world and the first person, male or female, to make the flight at the equator. As she told a friend, she felt she had one more good flight left in her. She hoped this was it.

FALSE START

A flight around the world called for much prep-
aration. A course had to be planned, maps prepared,
weather conditions studied. The plane had to be
equipped for the long flight. And AE would need a
navigator to help her find the way across long
stretches of ocean. While she worked on these
matters with a group of experts, GP was busy with
other arrangements. He had to clear permissions
for her to land in or fly over all the countries along
her route. He needed to arrange for supplies of
gasoline and spare parts along the route. And he
was in charge of raising money to pay for the flight.

The route AE decided on was from east to west:
Oakland to Hawaii to Howland to Australia to Arabia
to Africa to Brazil, and then home. Given the time

of year, weather conditions and winds should be favorable along that route.

As navigator, AE chose Captain Harry Manning of the SS *Roosevelt*. He was a good friend and captain of the ship on which she had returned from England in 1928. From Oakland to Australia, she would also have Fred Noonan, who had been a pilot and navigator for Pan American Airways. He was to relieve AE at the controls during long Pacific hops and to help with the navigation.

Paul Mantz was in charge of the plane. Among other things he made sure it had a range of 2,500

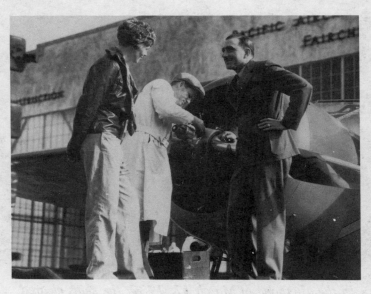

A mechanic works on the Electra as AE confers with Paul Manz, her chief adviser.

*In the afternoon of March 17, 1937, the skies cleared.
the Electra took off from Oakland and flew over the Bay
Bridge, heading westward.*

to 3,000 miles. He installed a Sperry Robot Pilot and spent hours training AE in a Link blind-flying trainer. He worried about whether she was being pushed too far too fast, whether she had the skills and strength for such a long flight. He was also worried that she might be starting out tired — in early 1937 she had delivered 136 lectures.

Many of AE's friends also had doubts about the flight, but none could talk her out of it. She believed that when one's time came, it came — and if it came she'd be doing what she most wanted to do.

By the morning of March 17, 1937, all was ready, but the day was rainy. About 4:30 P.M. the skies cleared. A short time later the Electra roared down the runway at Oakland and took off. On board were the three crew members and Paul Mantz, who was going along to visit his fiancee in Hawaii. The first leg of the trip went smoothly, and they landed in Hawaii some sixteen hours after takeoff.

The next leg was a long cross-ocean flight to the tiny island of Howland, where a landing strip had recently been built by the United States Government. The U.S. Coast Guard cutter *Itasca* would be standing by to offer any help needed. At the start of the trip, when everyone was fresh and with three of them aboard, it should not be hard to find this dot of land in the central Pacific.

Even so, AE was eager to put this part of the flight behind them. She wanted to snatch a few hours of rest and then push on to Howland. But a storm was moving in from the southwest. They would have to wait.

At dawn on March 20, the Electra was starting down the runway. Almost at once, AE felt the plane was sluggish. Halfway down the runway she knew they were in trouble — the plane was not going fast enough for liftoff. Suddenly it veered to the left. AE corrected. The plane made a sharp, uncontrollable turn. The landing gear collapsed and a wing was badly damaged. Gasoline poured onto the ground. Always cool-headed in emergencies, Amelia reached out and cut the switches so that no spark could set the gasoline ablaze.

No one was hurt, but the plane would not fly again until it had been sent to the mainland factory for repairs. These would take two months.

AE was still determined to make the flight. Even as the accident was taking place, she had said to herself, "If we don't burn up, I want to try again." Now everything had to be worked out a second time. The later starting date meant that weather patterns — storms and winds — would be different. AE would have to fly from west to east this time. She would need new maps and charts, new stores of gasoline and spare parts.

The delay also meant that Harry Manning would have to return to his ship instead of making the flight. AE asked Fred Noonan to make the whole

AE flew the plane. GP was in charge of raising funds, clearing permissions to land, and making sure gasoline and parts were available.

trip with her. He was highly skilled and had years of experience, but Pan American had let him go because of his drinking. Amelia knew about his problem. But she believed that people could change, and she trusted Fred when he told her that he had sworn off alcohol. The flight was, as they both knew, his chance for a comeback. He was newly married and eager to succeed.

In mid-May repairs were finished on the Electra. AE tested it, then flew from Burbank to Oakland to pick up Fred. They were headed for Miami, the takeoff point. Here the Electra would receive its final check-up.

AE at the controls of the Electra.

Paul Mantz was upset when he learned that Amelia had left for Miami. He was not satisfied with the radio equipment or AE's knowledge of how to spin out her fuel.

Amelia waited a week in Miami while Pan American experts went over the plane. The radio equipment gave the experts endless problems.

The plane's radio could be used both with voice and telegraph key, for sending and receiving. AE planned to use a frequency of 6210 kilocycles to send by voice during the day and a frequency of 3105 to send by night.

The Electra was also equipped with a radio

direction finder. The direction finder, or DF, was a recent invention and used in navigation. It was meant to let fliers pick up a stream of radio signals and home in on the source. Paul Mantz thought a DF might be very useful if AE and Fred found themselves in fog or clouds. During their flight to Howland, the *Itasca* would send out signals for them to home in on.

The DF, however, did not work well on the high frequencies AE was planning to use for sending by voice. For that reason, the radio equipment had been adapted so that they could also send and receive on 500 kilocycles. This would make radio direction finding much easier. But to use 500 kilocycles, they would need a training wire antenna at least 250 feet long to strengthen the signals.

AE hated reeling an antenna in and out, but Paul had had one installed on the plane. Without it, AE would be out of touch with homing signals for hours at a time.

At last the experts were satisfied with the plane and the radio equipment. On June 1 Amelia got up in the dark of early morning and drove out to Miami airport with George. By 5 A.M. she and Fred were aboard the plane. George leaned in the cockpit to say good-bye. Minutes later, the Electra took off into a cloudless sky.

Left behind were the telegraph key and the trailing antenna.

AROUND THE WORLD

AE and Fred had learned to fly at a time when planes were much simpler. Both had mixed feelings about all the new instruments. They knew these were supposed to make flying safer. But Fred had had bad experiences with direction finders that were not working properly. He did not trust them. AE thought that watching all the new dials and gauges in the cockpit caused the pilot's eyes to tire. Neither one was really at home with radio — or convinced that radio was helpful. They left the telegraph key behind because neither of them could send or read Morse. They did not see what use it would be to them. No one has ever been sure who had the wire antenna removed.

In any case, they were off at last, heading for San Juan, Puerto Rico, where they would spend the

Fred (left) and AE have lunch at the airport of a small oil town in Venezuela.

night. AE put the plane on automatic pilot and looked down, enjoying the sight of rocks and reefs poking up through the water, of islands and the shadows of clouds. She began to make notes. She was under contract to write articles for a newspaper and send them in from various stops. She was also keeping a log to send home from time to time. At the end of the trip she planned to put everything together and write a book.

The trip wore on, to Venezuela and Dutch Guiana. They stopped in Brazil for two days while Pan American's mechanics overhauled the Electra before the long hop over the Atlantic — 1,900 miles to West Africa and the French colonial city of Dakar.

After leaving Brazil, they flew into heavy rain. It pounded so hard that AE could feel the plane shaking. Then the weather cleared and they flew on in calm skies. AE put the plane on automatic pilot, which she found a great help. On her last crossing of the Atlantic, she had had to keep her hand on the stick for the entire flight.

A thick haze blurred the coast of West Africa as they approached. At his chart table in the cabin, Fred worked out their position and wrote AE a note, telling her when to turn south for Dakar. He attached the note to the end of the fishing pole they carried for this purpose and passed it up to her. Amelia read it and shook her head. Instinct told her to turn north and she did so, believing that Fred had made an error. A town appeared, and she landed. It was not Dakar. That city lay to the south, as Fred had told her.

The next day they flew to Dakar, where the plane was thoroughly overhauled. They were about to fly 4,350 miles across Africa, making four stops. It was a trip that took them over vast stretches of jungles, over mountains and plains, and over deserts with no landmarks. At the end they flew down the coast of Eritrea to Assab, where a large supply of gasoline had been stored. Their next stop was 2,000 miles away — Karachi, which was then part of

India. This long leg would have to be flown non-stop because they had been refused permission to land in Saudi Arabia.

From Karachi they went on to Calcutta, where the airfield was waterlogged and the Electra's wheels sent up fountains of spray. The monsoon season was about to start, and they hoped to squeeze through before the stormy rains began in earnest.

By morning a night's rain had made the field wetter than ever. Takeoff would be tricky — but more rains were on the way. With the wet soil sucking at its wheels and sticking to them, the Electra roared down the runway more slowly than AE liked. At the last moment the plane lifted and barely cleared the fringe of trees that surrounded the airfield.

AE and Fred stopped briefly in Akyab, Burma, for refueling. Then they took off for Rangoon, where they planned to spend the night. In almost no time they ran into a wall of black clouds. Within the clouds, head winds battered the plane. Rain slashed at it, peeling patches of paint off the leading edges of the wings. It was impossible to see. For two hours they tried to find a way through or out of the storm clouds. In the end they had to turn back to Akyab, flying blind. Fred managed to find the way. They reached Rangoon the next day.

By the time they reached Bangkok, Thailand, the weather was fair and so they pressed on to Singapore the same day. From there they flew to Bandung, Java, where the plane was serviced. The next day, June 24, they had planned a long hop to Port Darwin, Australia, but one of the instruments Fred needed was not working properly. They were delayed while technicians worked on it and decided to fly to Surabaya, which was much closer than Port Darwin. On the way, however, Fred found that the instrument still was not working properly, and so they turned back. Two days later they were able to leave for Timor and then for Port Darwin.

Now the long cross-ocean flights were coming up. The Electra was carefully serviced and a blown fuse was replaced in the radio direction finder. AE and Fred lightened the plane by sending home everything they did not need. Among these things were their parachutes, which would not be much help over the Pacific.

The flight to Lae, New Guinea, was an eight-hour battle against head winds. They arrived at 3 P.M., tired from the struggle and also deeply weary from all the miles of flying that lay behind them. They had come 22,000 miles in only a month, making 30 stops in 19 countries on 5 continents, often in wind, rain, and thunderstorms. But tired or not, AE was eager to finish, to complete the last 7,000 miles. She wanted to be home by the Fourth of July and well ahead of her fortieth birthday. She hoped to take off the next day.

Lae was an ideal jumping-off spot. It was head-quarters for the Guinea Airways Company, which flew Lockheed planes that were sister craft to the Electra. Service on the plane was excellent. There was also a local hotel with good food, hot baths, and comfortable beds. But the people who had dinner with Fred found that he was drinking heavily and complaining that Amelia was pushing too hard.

By early morning the Electra had been serviced and fueled, but the wind was blowing in the wrong direction and clouds were building up. Even more important, Fred had not been able to check the time shown by his chronometer, the very precise clock he needed for navigating. Neither the Electra's radio nor the receivers at Lae had been able to pick up the exact-time signals broadcast by the U.S. Navy and the Bureau of Standards.

Like all chronometers, the Electra's lost or gained a few seconds a day. Fred needed to know how far off exact time it was. Then he could allow for that when calculating their position. Tiny differences between the time shown on the chronometer and exact time could add up to big errors. A difference of only fifteen seconds would mean an error of one mile. A difference of one minute would mean an error of four miles when Fred calculated where they were. In a flight of 2,600 miles, the wrong time could put them far off course.

On AE's earlier ocean-crossing flights, she had

been aiming at continents. She didn't always come down where she thought she would, but she did find land. Howland Island, however, was two miles long and a half mile wide. Its highest point was twenty feet above sea level. Also, Howland was in the middle of a large ocean. If they became lost, there would be no roads, railroad tracks, or rivers to follow, no place to put down and ask for directions. It would take accurate instruments and all Fred's skill to find Howland.

Whether Fred could exercise his skills would depend on the weather. He could not navigate by the stars if the skies were cloudy and overcast. In that case they would have to depend on radio. And without the trailing antenna, their range for sending and receiving would be about 500 miles. For much of the 2,600-mile flight, they would be out of touch with both Lae and Howland.

While waiting to get off, AE and Fred did some sightseeing. They also repacked the plane and lightened it still more with a final cleaning out of everything they thought they did not absolutely have to have.

The next morning at 10 A.M. they took off on the most dangerous part of the whole trip, heading for a dot of land in the central Pacific. They never found it.

LAST FLIGHT

AE's original plan was to follow the most direct route from Lae to Howland. Most of the time she would be out of touch with radio operators on land. So a Navy ship, the USS *Ontario,* had been stationed halfway along the route. It was to radio information about the weather when the Electra passed overhead during the night. AE expected to be nearing Howland by dawn and homing in on radio signals from the Coast Guard cutter *Itasca.*

While at Lae, however, she had made a change in the plan, as suggested by Harry Balfour, the radio operator for Guinea Airways. He was worried about the flight, wanted to help, and thought a slightly different route would be better.

The new route led to the Nukumanu Islands, 750 miles east of Lae. AE could find these by using other islands as landmarks and would arrive just before sunset. She was then to turn northeast for Nauru Island, which had a bright new lighthouse. It also had a phosphate mine with bright lights. Harry arranged for these lights to be turned on all night. By the time she passed Nauru, AE would be a little more than halfway to Howland.

There would be no more check points. But even if the night was cloudy, by early morning Fred should be able to get a sun line, which would give him a good idea of their longitude. He could then calculate how far west of Howland they were. But this information would not tell them whether they were on course. They might be either north or south of the island.

Both the original course and the new one called for AE to fly over the British-held Gilbert Islands during the night. The British had radio transmitters on two of the islands, but they had not been asked to help guide the Electra. Nonetheless, AE knew the Gilberts were on her route. If for some reason, she could not find Howland, her plan was to turn back and head for the Gilberts.

Harry Balfour and AE last talked by radio when she turned northeast for Nauru. She was heard on Nauru as she passed over the island. After that came hours of silence and darkness.

Miles away the Coast Guard cutter *Itasca* was standing by, near Howland Island. In early evening word had arrived that AE and Fred were on their way. Captain and crew were ready for the long night ahead. Searchlights went on at midnight, sweeping the sky. They would serve as a beacon for the incoming plane, in case it picked up a tailwind and arrived early. The boilers were fully stoked, ready to give off thick black clouds of smoke by day. Radio messages had been sent and received by the *Itasca.* These showed that the transmitters and receivers were working well.

The *Itasca* had a direction finder with a range of 550 to 270 kilocycles. Ashore, on Howland, a second DF had been installed. This was an exper-

The U.S. Coast Guard cutter Itasca *was standing by at Howland.*

imental, high-frequency DF, on loan from the Navy.

So the *Itasca* was equipped to send signals that AE could pick up and home in on. The DFs on Howland and the *Itasca* could pick up signals from the Electra and locate the plane. This information could then be radioed to AE by voice.

There were limits, however, to what a direction finder could do. It could only pick up certain frequencies. The signals had to be strong. And they had to last at least two minutes for the operator to do his job.

When signals were coming in, the operator rotated a loop antenna. The radio signals were strongest when the loop was lined up with them. They were weakest when the sides of the loop were 90 degrees away from them. The weakest signals were easier to fine-tune than the strongest. So the operator rotated the loop to find the weakest reception, which was called a minimum or a null. He could then get a fix on the source — it was 90 degrees away from the minimum.

The arrangement was that the *Itasca* would send homing signals and weather reports on the hour and the half hour. At quarter to and quarter after each hour, AE would send her call letters, KHAQQ, and any other flight information she wished to give.

At midnight the *Itasca* began sending by voice and by telegraph key. No one aboard knew that AE and Fred could not read Morse — and no one knew that the Electra's telegraph key and trailing wire antenna had been left behind in Miami.

At 12:30 A.M. the ship broadcast again: wind direction east, force 11 miles, partly cloudy, visibility 20 miles, calm swell, direction east.

By 1:15 AE had still not been heard from, but this was not surprising. She was probably too far out to be heard. At 1:30 the ship radioed AE that it had not heard from her and asked that she "please observe schedule with key." The minutes ticked away without an answer. The *Itasca* went on transmitting on the hour and half hour.

At 2:45 the radio room began to crackle with static. The listeners strained toward the loudspeaker. They heard AE's voice calmly reporting on 3105 kilocycles, "Cloudy and overcast." The rest of the message was lost in static.

At 3 A.M. the *Itasca* sent the weather report: clear skies, ceiling unlimited, wind east at eight miles per hour. It then began sending out by key the dit-dah of the letter *A*, the signal that was supposed to guide the Electra to Howland.

Three-fifteen brought no word from the plane.

At 3:30 *Itasca* again sent the weather and asked AE to report her position and estimated time of arrival at Howland on her next broadcast.

AE came in at 3:45, reporting by voice, "*Itasca* from Earhart . . . *Itasca* from Earhart . . . Overcast . . . Will listen on hour and half hour on 3105 . . .

Will listen on hour and half hour on 3105."

The *Itasca* went on sending and listening. Just before 5 A.M. AE was heard, but no one could make out what she was saying. She was next heard from at 6:15. By then she had been flying for almost eighteen hours and had about another four hours of fuel. She asked the *Itasca* to take a bearing on her. She would whistle into her microphone, she said, so the direction finder could get a fix on her position. She added that she was "about two hundred miles out," with no landfall in sight.

The whistle was lost in static.

A half hour later, AE's voice came through clear and strong. "Please take a bearing on us, and report in half an hour. I will make a noise in the microphone. About one hundred miles out." But she was on the air too briefly.

For nearly an hour the *Itasca* kept signaling, sending messages, and asking AE to reply. The men in the radio room grew more and more tense.

At 7:42 AE broke in, saying, "We must be on you, but cannot see you. But gas is running low. Been unable to reach you by radio. We are flying at altitude 1,000 feet."

The *Itasca* replied immediately. AE's signal strength was so strong that she could not be far away.

At 7:58 AE called in again, her voice loud and clear. "KHAQQ calling *Itasca*," she said. "We are circling, but cannot hear you. Go ahead on 7500 either now or on schedule time of half hour."

The *Itasca* sent out a long series of *A*s on 7500 kilocycles.

AE answered, "We are receiving your signals, but are unable to get a minimum. Please take a bearing on us and answer with voice on 3105." Again she whistled. And again the whistle was lost in static.

By now it was more than clear that there were problems with the Electra's radio equipment. AE had not received most of the ship's messages and could not get a bearing from the homing signals. All the *Itasca* could do was to go on sending.

At 8:45 AE was heard clearly. "We are on line of position 157 dash 337," she said. "Will repeat this message on 6210 kilocycles. Wait, listening on 6210 kilocycles. We are running north and south."

But "We are running north and south" were the last words the *Itasca* ever heard from AE.

Ten A.M. was the time when the Electra would probably run out of fuel. Minutes later the search for Amelia Earhart and Fred Noonan got under way. Around Howland and to the south and east, the weather was fair. About fifty miles to the north and west were heavy cloud banks. The radio static was one sign that the Electra had been in stormy weather. AE's failure to see the *Itasca*'s searchlights or billowing black smoke was another. The *Itasca* headed northwest.

Within hours, the largest sea search in the history

MISS EARHART FORCED DOWN AT SEA, HOWLAND ISLE FEARS; COAST GUARD BEGINS SEARCH

FUEL HAD RUN LOW

Fliers Were Near Goal When Last Reported but Saw No Land

PLANE EQUIPPED TO FLOAT

Has Sealed Gasoline Tanks and a Rubber Lifeboat for Emergency at Sea

RADIO BELIEVED HEARD

Los Angeles Amateurs Pick Up Weak Signals on Frequency Assigned to the Plane

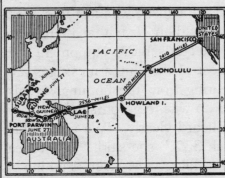

ROUTE OF EARHART PLANE IN PACIFIC

The flier took off from Lae, New Guinea, at 8 P. M., New York time, Thursday, and was in the vicinity of Howland Island at 4:43 P. M. Friday, when she was in communication with the Coast Guard cutter Itasca. She had intended to fly from this island to Honolulu and thence to the mainland for the completion of her world tour.

By The Associated Press.

WASHINGTON, July 2. — Coast Guard headquarters was advised tonight that Amelia Earhart was believed to have alighted on the Pacific Ocean near Howland Island shortly after 5 P. M. Eastern daylight time today.

A message from the cutter Itasca, stationed in the vicinity of the island in the mid-Pacific, said:

"Earhart unreported at Howland at 7 P. M. [E. D. T.]. Believe down shortly after 5 P. M. Am searching probable area and will continue."

Admiral William D. Leahy, chief of naval operations, instructed the commandant of the naval station at Honolulu tonight to render whatever aid he may deem practicable in the search for Miss Earhart.

Plane Joins in Search

[A navy flying boat hopped off from Honolulu late last night for Howland Island, 1,900 miles dis-

SOVIET 'LIQUIDATES' 120 MORE AS SPIES

Disclosure Indicates Others May Have Been Shot as the Agents of Estonia and Poland

AVIATOR IS AMONG THEM

Government Is Now Trying to Check Persecution of the Innocent in Campaign

Wireless to THE NEW YORK TIMES.

MOSCOW, July 2.— The detection and "liquidation" of two large

VALERA FAR AHEAD IN IRISH ELECTION

His Return to Power in Dail Seems Assured by Early Count in Free State

VOTE ON CHARTER CLOSE

Heavy Adverse Sentiment Is Indicated—Larkin, Labor Leader, Wins Seat

Special Cable to THE NEW YORK TIMES.

DUBLIN, Irish Free State, July 3. — The first returns in the Free State of the U.S. Navy was being organized. President Roosevelt ordered all available men, ships, and planes to take part. In the days that followed, the search force grew until it included a battleship, four destroyers, a minesweeper, a seaplane, and planes of the aircraft carrier *Lexington,* which had sailed for Howland from San Francisco. In all, ships and planes searched 250,000 square miles of the Pacific.

At first, hopes ran high that AE and Fred would be found. Perhaps the plane was being kept afloat by its empty fuel tanks. Or perhaps the two fliers were safe in a rubber raft. Or perhaps they had been picked up by one of the Japanese fishing boats that were in the area. Radio messages were received, with the call letters KHAQQ. Most turned out to be cruel hoaxes that raised false hopes. With each passing day chances grew slimmer that AE and Fred would be found. Finally, on July 19, the search was called off. No trace of the fliers or their plane had been discovered.

What had gone wrong? The most likely explanation seemed to be the cloudy, overcast weather that AE had reported. With Fred unable to see the stars, they had somehow got off course. There may have been trouble with the navigation instruments. Certainly there was trouble with the radio equipment. In early morning, Fred had apparently been able to take a bearing on the sun; the best guess was that "line of position 157 dash 337" was a sun line. It told them that they were on a line with Howland but they did not know whether they were north or south of the island. So they were circling and running north and south.

The clouds to the northwest had marked stormy weather. On the day of their disappearance, the Navy had sent a long-distance seaplane from Hawaii to help with the search. Its pilot flew into extremely bad weather north of Howland — snow, sleet, rain, and electrical storms between 2,000 and 12,000 feet. The cloud tops appeared to be at 18,000 feet or higher. If AE met that same storm, she could not have flown above it. If she had to ditch below it, waves would have destroyed the Electra almost at once.

It was possible, however, that AE had enough fuel to go on flying until noon or even 2 P.M., if she was careful. If so, there was a good chance that she might have tried to reach the Gilbert Islands. But no trace of AE, Fred, or the Electra was found among the Gilberts.

The official conclusion was that Amelia Earhart and Fred Noonan had been lost at sea.

But there was no proof of this — no bodies, no wreckage. To many people the disappearance was an unsolved mystery. Then, as now, some people thought the key to the mystery could be found in an area the Navy had not been allowed to search: Pacific islands controlled by Japan.

PRISONERS OF THE JAPANESE?

The western Pacific has several groups of small islands, among them the Marshalls, the Carolines, and the Marianas. In 1937 these islands were in Japanese hands.

Japan did not own the islands, although it wanted to. It had been put in charge of them by the peace conference that followed World War I. It was forbidden to fortify the islands or to use them for military purposes, but it was doing so anyway.

The Japanese meant to control Asia and the western Pacific. They had already attacked China. And they had been preparing the islands for war — deepening harbors, building docks, roads, and airfields, putting in fuel storage tanks and ammunition dumps. To keep their work secret, they did not allow foreign ships to dock or foreign planes to land.

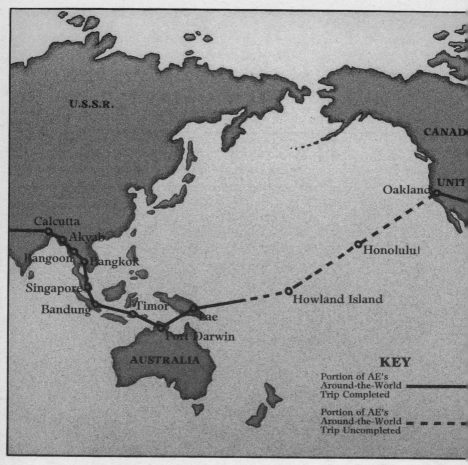

Map labels:
U.S.S.R.
CANAD[A]
UNIT[ED]
Oakland
Honolulu
Calcutta
Akyab
Rangoon
Bangkok
Singapore
Bandung
Timor
Lae
Port Darwin
Howland Island
AUSTRALIA

KEY

Portion of AE's
Around-the-World
Trip Completed

Portion of AE's
Around-the-World
Trip Uncompleted

They suspected all foreigners of being spies. Many were arrested and some were put to death.

When Amelia Earhart and Fred Noonan disappeared, the United States asked Japan for permission to search for them among the islands. The Japanese refused, saying they would search for the fliers themselves. Planes and ships of the U.S. Navy

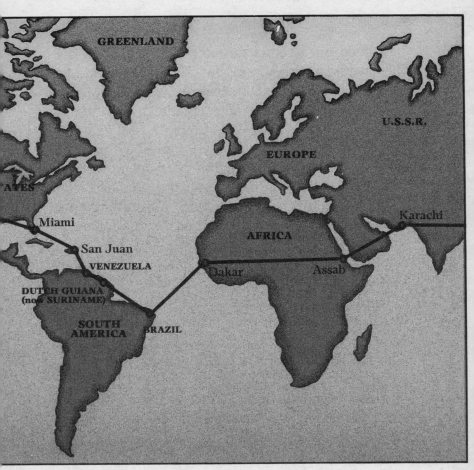

kept away. No one wanted to risk starting a war.

The Japanese said they had found no trace of the fliers. Perhaps because no one else had found a trace either, rumors began to spread. The most widespread was that AE and Fred had been captured by the Japanese — they had been shot down and were being held as spies. Perhaps, people said, they had been on a secret mission — even though the fliers would have been over the islands in the middle of the night and had no way of seeing or photographing anything. A movie made during World War II helped to keep the rumors alive. The film told of a famous woman flier who agreed to "become lost" over the Pacific so that Navy planes could search for her and photograph the Japanese-run islands. The flier was really to go into hiding on a small island. But when she learned that the Japanese knew of the plan and would pick her up on the island, she crashed her plane into the Pacific so that a search could take place anyway.

During and after the war, U.S. forces in the Pacific were asked to watch for prisoners on the islands. Now new rumors started. Servicemen met natives who had heard about a white woman flier and a white man with a bandage on his head. The two had crash-landed, been picked up by a Japanese ship, and taken away. In some stories they had later died of disease; in others they had been executed as spies.

The stories did not seem to lead anywhere. And then one story came to light that gave new life to all the rumors. It was a story that appeared in a California newspaper, and it was told by a woman named Josephine Blanco Akiyama.

Mrs. Akiyama was a native of Saipan, an island in the Marianas that had been a headquarters for the Japanese. After the war she worked as an assistant to a dentist in the U.S. Navy. In 1957 she and her husband moved to California. Her story had to do with something she had seen as a young girl on Saipan in the summer of 1937. She was sure of the year, she said, because it was the one when she graduated from the Japanese school she had been attending. She was eleven years old.

One day she was riding her bicycle toward Tanapag harbor, taking lunch to her brother-in-law, who worked in a military area there. She heard a plane flying overhead. She thought it was in some kind of trouble, because it came in low and belly-landed in the harbor.

A short time later, the workers were buzzing with excitement. "Come and see the American woman," everyone was saying. Josephine Blanco joined them. She was surprised to see a white woman who had short hair and was wearing a shirt and trousers, like a man. With the woman was a tall white man wearing a short-sleeved shirt. Soldiers led the couple away to a clearing in the woods. Shots rang out. Then the soldiers returned alone.

Josephine Blanco had first told her story to the Navy dentist with whom she worked. Later in California she saw photographs of Amelia Earhart and Fred Noonan. She thought they looked like the couple she had seen as a girl on Saipan. She told her story again.

The story raised some questions. First, was it true? Newspaper reporters found the former Navy dentist in New Jersey. Yes, he said, he remembered Josephine Blanco's story. He had been talking with a fellow dentist one day about the disappearance of Amelia Earhart, when Josephine Blanco interrupted to tell what she had seen. He could not think of a reason for her to have invented the story. She had surely seen something.

Could the two people have been Amelia Earhart and Fred Noonan? There cannot have been many white couples flying around Saipan in 1937. If the couple were flying the plane, they were almost certainly AE and Fred. But if they arrived in a Japanese seaplane, they could have been AE and Fred or they could have been two other people.

Could AE and Fred have landed at Saipan? This seems almost impossible, no matter what the weather was like. A Saipan landing would mean that after passing Nauru, they turned the plane around and flew northwest. A compass alone would have told them they were heading in the wrong direction.

If they were ever on Saipan, they were taken there, either by ship or by plane. Had they ever been on Saipan?

One of the people who tried to answer that question was Fred Goerner, a CBS radio broad-caster. Over six years he made four trips to Saipan and interviewed hundreds of people. He interviewed former servicemen in the United States. He made trips to Washington, D.C., hoping to find clues to the mystery in government files. At one time, he thought he had found the grave of AE and Fred, but it was not theirs. Another time he thought he had found the generator from the Electra, but it was from another plane. When he finally gave up, he wrote a book, *The Search for Amelia Earhart.*

Another person who tried to answer the question was Vincent Loomis, a retired Air Force officer who read Goerner's book and took up the search. He, too, interviewed hundreds of people on Saipan and also in the Marshall Islands and Japan. Later he, too, wrote a book: *Amelia Earhart: The Final Story.*

The research done by Goerner and Loomis shows that Amelia Earhart's last flight may have ended like this.

After leaving Nauru, AE and Fred flew on into cloudy, overcast weather. Fred could not navigate by the stars. They followed their compasses but got off course. Perhaps winds blew them off course. Perhaps the plane drifted to the north — other fliers had noted that AE tended to drift to the left. Perhaps AE, following instinct, turned north, as she had when approaching West Africa. About the time they should have been reaching Howland, they were north of the island and in stormy weather. The radio equipment was not working well, and the storm made it worse. They thought they were near Howland and tried to find it by circling and running north and south. But they could not.

At last, with only two or three hours of fuel left, they decided to try for the Gilbert Islands. Fred made his best guess as to where they were and laid out a course. AE followed it. But because they did not realize they were well north of Howland, the course was wrong. It led them not to the Gilberts but to the Japanese-run Marshall Islands.

After circling, AE set the plane down as best she could in shallow water. Fred was injured in the crash-landing but AE was not. They reached shore, believing themselves safely in the Gilberts — and soon found themselves prisoners of the Japanese, arrested as spies.

A Japanese cargo ship arrived. The prisoners were taken aboard. Their plane, with one wing broken, was hoisted out of the water in a canvas sling onto the ship. The two were taken to the island of Jaluit. There the wounds on Fred's head and leg were treated by a medical corpsman of the Japanese Navy. After questioning, AE and Fred were taken to Saipan, perhaps by seaplane to the harbor at Tanapag, where Josephine Blanco saw them. On Saipan they were kept in prison until they died of disease or were executed. They had seen too much military activity. The Japanese could not let them go.

Japanese records show that no search of the islands was ever made for AE and Fred. It would not have been needed if the fliers had already been found.

The story pieced together by Goerner and Loomis is a strong one. But it may or may not be the true story of what happened. The people they interviewed were talking about events that took place twenty to forty years earlier. Memories fade. Fact becomes mixed with fiction. People try to give the answers they think are wanted. Also, many of the people interviewed had heard about the fliers, not seen them.

So far, there is no evidence that backs up the stories — no official documents, no photographs, no bones, no wreckage, no person with whom the white prisoners talked.

That is why the mystery goes on, fifty or more years after AE and Fred disappeared. It is possible that they crash-landed in the Marshalls and died on Saipan. It is equally possible that they crash-landed in the stormy Pacific and that the Lockheed Electra sank within seconds, as the Navy and the Coast Guard thought.

AE understood the dangers of her flights. She never really thought she would live to grow old. And she had said more than once, "When I go, I'd like best to go in my plane. Quickly."

Her friends always hoped that she got her wish. They could not bear to think that she died of disease, caged in a prison.

LOST STAR

The symbol of the Lockheed Company is a winged star, and the company has named many of its planes after stars or constellations — Vega, Sirius, Altair, Orion. In the middle 1930s, the company needed a name for its newest plane. Researchers went to the library, read books, and found something they liked.

This was a Greek myth that told of the Pleiades, the seven daughters of Atlas. As young women they were pursued through the forest by the hunter Orion. The great god Jupiter took pity on them and changed them first to doves and then to a group of stars, the constellation we call the Pleiades.

In the beginning there were seven stars — the seven sisters. But the one named Electra could not bear to see her beloved city of Troy perish in the flames of war. She tore herself away from her sisters and became a comet. And that is why, said the myth, only six stars are clearly visible in the Pleiades. One star was lost, Electra.

Lockheed decided to name its new plane Electra, lost star and bright comet.

Amelia Earhart made her last flight in an Electra. Like the plane's namesake, she became a lost star. And in a career that lasted only nine years she lighted up the sky and then, like a comet, disappeared from sight.

Further Reading

All of these are adult books, but they are easy reading. Some of them are old books; some were printed in small editions. If the books are not in your library, it may be possible to borrow what you want through the interlibrary loan system. Ask your librarian.

Briand, Paul L., Jr., *Daughter of the Sky, The Story of Amelia Earhart.* New York: Duell, Sloan and Pearce, 1960.

Earhart, Amelia (arranged by George Palmer Putnam), *Last Flight.* New York: Harcourt, Brace & Company, 1937.

Earhart, Amelia, *The Fun of It.* New York: Harcourt, Brace and Company, 1932. Reprint edition, Chicago: Academy Press, 1977, 1978, 1984.

Earhart, Amelia, *20 Hrs. 40 Min.* New York: G. P. Putnam's Sons, 1928. Reprint edition, New York: Arno Press, 1980.

Loomis, Vincent, with Jeffrey Ethell, *Amelia Earhart: The Final Story.* New York: Random House, 1985.

Moolman, Valerie, *Women Aloft.* Alexandria, Virginia: Time-Life Books, 1981.

Morrissey, Muriel Earhart, *Courage Is the Price.* Wichita, Kansas: McCormick-Armstrong Publishing Division, 1963.

Putnam, George Palmer, *Soaring Wings.* New York: Harcourt, Brace & Company, 1939.